Nicky
The Swamp Dog
A TRUE STORY

Story by
JACKLYN SONNIER HIRSHBERG

Photography by
D. RAY GUILLORY

Acadian House
PUBLISHING
LAFAYETTE, LOUISIANA

Library of Congress Cataloging-in-Publication Data

Hirshberg, Jacklyn Sonnier, 1949-
     Nicky the swamp dog : a true story / story by Jacklyn Sonnier Hirshberg;
photography by D. Ray Guillory.
     p. cm.
     ISBN 0-925417-36-X
     1. Rat terrier—Louisiana—Atchafalaya River Region—Biography—Juvenile literature.
     2. Atchafalaya River (La.)—Description and travel—Juvenile literature.
     3. Swamps—Louisiana—Atchafalaya River Region—Juvenile literature.
     4. Guillory, D. Ray, 1950—Juvenile literature. [1. Rat terrier. 2. Dogs.
        3. Atchafalaya River (La.)—Description and travel. 4. Swamps—
        Louisiana—Atchafalaya River Region. 5. Guillory, D. Ray, 1950-]
     I. Guillory, D. Ray, 1950- ill. II. Title.
     SF429.R35 H55 2000
     636.755'092'9—dc21
                         00-010254

♦ **Published by Acadian House Publishing, Lafayette, Louisiana
    (Edited by Trent Angers; interior graphic design by Jon Russo)**

♦ **Cover design by Michelle Marse, Lafayette, Louisiana**

♦ **Color separations by Saturn Graphics, Lafayette, Louisiana**

♦ **Printed by Walsworth Press, Marceline, Missouri**

This book is dedicated to all of God's creatures that live in the great Atchafalaya River Basin . . . and to the human visitors who have come to respect and appreciate the natural beauty of this special little corner of the world.

Acknowledgements

The author thanks her mother, Martha Sonnier, and her daughter, Eva Hirshberg, for encouraging her in this project when the going got tough; and her husband, Dr. Richard Hirshberg, who listened patiently to her many, many tales of adventure in the swamp.

The photographer thanks his parents, Ray and Bernice Guillory, who always allowed him the freedom to roam the great outdoors of southeast Texas and who nurtured his love for God's beautiful creation.

The author and photographer also thank the talented staff of Acadian House Publishing, especially the editor, Trent Angers, who spent countless hours working with the text and carefully selecting the photographs from the hundreds that were submitted.

About the Author...

JACKLYN SONNIER HIRSHBERG is an anthropologist who studied at the University of Houston, focusing on the culture of Native American Indians. After living in Houston for 25 years, she returned to her hometown of Lafayette, Louisiana, and was introduced to the nearby Atchafalaya River Basin, which she now considers "The Eighth Wonder of the World."

A tour of the swamp with guide D. Ray "Half Pint" Guillory in the summer of 1997 developed into a two-year course of learning about the basin and the variety of wildlife which inhabits this vast semi-wilderness area.

About the Photographer...

D. RAY "HALF PINT" GUILLORY is a swamp guide who lives with his dog, Nicky, in a houseboat in the Atchafalaya River Basin near Henderson, Louisiana. He got his nickname, "Half Pint," only because he was smaller than his brother. Born in Orange, Texas, in 1950, he spent his childhood roaming the wooded areas, rice fields and swamps near his home. Feeling right at home in the great outdoors, he became a self-taught naturalist and photographer.

After living in the wilderness of southeast Texas for two decades, he moved to the Atchafalaya swamp in the mid-1980s. Operating under the banner of "Half Pint's Small Boat Swamp Adventures," he has taken visitors from all over the world into the swamp to show them an environment such as they had never seen before.

He trained Nicky to help entertain visitors to the swamp; he also taught her to rescue lost or injured animals. He considers his little swamp dog to be his best friend.

Table of Contents

Attracted by the mystery of the swamp

It was in the summer of 1997 that I first met the swamp guide, "Half Pint" Guillory, and his amazing little friend, Nicky.

I had just returned home to Lafayette, Louisiana, after living in Houston, Texas, for 25 years. I wanted to get away from the hustle and bustle of the big city, to come home to the relative peace and quiet of the smaller city where I grew up.

I was looking forward to driving around the countryside, seeing the bayous and sugarcane fields, and maybe attending some of the festivals for which south Louisiana is famous.

And, for some reason, I had a strong desire to see the swamp. Maybe it was because I never went into the swamp when I was growing up. Maybe it was because I had a feeling there was something special waiting for me, something magical to be discovered, if only I would venture out.

I wasn't interested in seeing the swamp in a large tour boat. I wanted to see it up close and personal, in a smaller boat with a guide who was as familiar with the swamp as I was with my own backyard.

After several days of asking around, I located Half Pint. A sign on his houseboat read "Half Pint's Small Boat Swamp Adventures." I learned from those who knew him that he had spent most of his adult life in the wilderness of southeast Texas and the swamps of south Louisiana.

He was at home in the swamp. He was a genuine swamp guide, "The Real McCoy," as the old folks would say.

And he had the cutest little dog that he was training to be his "assistant." He was teaching Nicky to find and rescue lost or injured animals, such as beavers, nutria and owls.

I took my first trip into the swamp with Half Pint and Nicky. I was intrigued with all the wildlife we saw that day, including great white birds that seemed to be everywhere, plus beavers, hawks and alligators of every size. I knew then and there that I wanted to learn everything I possibly could about the swamp. So, I started going with them on the boat three days a week as they took visitors into the swamp. Then I went five days a week and started helping with the tours. I did this for nearly two years.

Throughout this period I learned a lot about the swamp. And I gained a deep appreciation for the beauty of the great outdoors. Being with Half Pint and Nicky made the experience all the more special.

It is an experience I want to share with as many people as possible, and that is why I wrote this book.

So, come with me to the Atchafalaya River Basin and meet my two best friends.

– *Jackie Hirshberg*

Nicky
The Swamp Dog
— A TRUE STORY —

CHAPTER ONE

The Puppy Finds a Home

Once there was a little black and white and brown puppy who didn't have a home. She didn't even have a name.

She was born on a sugarcane farm in south Louisiana. She had five other brothers and sisters. The man who owned the farm liked all the puppies but he couldn't afford to keep them, so he gave them away to other people who could take care of them.

One of the farmer's friends, who lived on a levee near a fishing village called Henderson, agreed to help by finding a home for the little black and white and brown puppy. One of his neighbors was a nice man named Half Pint who just might want the puppy.

Everyone in the neighborhood knew Half Pint was very kind to animals. He would find sick or injured animals in the swamp and take them home and nurse them back to health.

◁ *The puppy's new home: a houseboat in the Atchafalaya River Basin at Henderson, Louisiana.*

So Half Pint's neighbor was pretty sure that Half Pint would fall in love with the homeless puppy as soon as he saw her.

The man put the puppy in a small cardboard box, got into his truck, and drove down the levee to Half Pint's home. As soon as Half Pint saw the puppy, he agreed to adopt her.

The little dog was so small that she could fit into a cereal

bowl. She had a big head that seemed too big for such a tiny dog. She had big, pointy ears and big, round brown eyes. And a little pink tongue.

Her new master was a tall man with a silver beard. He had kind, blue eyes and he wore glasses. He lived on a houseboat near the levee, on the edge of the great Atchafalaya River swamp. He was a swamp guide; his job was to take visitors out on his tour boat to see the swamp and the animals that live there. His business was called "Half Pint's Small Boat Swamp Adventures."

"What's your name, little gal?" Half Pint asked the puppy. "No name, huh? Cat got your tongue?"

Half Pint picked up the puppy and held her in the palm of his hand. She looked up at her new master as though she was waiting to hear the name he was about to give her.

"Well, let's see. Christmas is right around the corner, and

Above: *The levee which borders the Atchafalaya River Basin is beautiful in the springtime.* **Left:** *Nicky enjoys running down the levee near her new home.*

it's time for Saint Nicholas to come and bring presents. You are like a present to me, so I think I'll call you Nicky, after Saint Nick. How's that? Nicky. Nicky, the swamp dog."

Half Pint

The puppy seemed to like the name. Half Pint was pleased with the selection, as well.

"I hope you like your new home," Half Pint said as he folded a plaid blanket and laid it on the wooden floor in a corner of the houseboat. "This will be your bed."

Half Pint placed Nicky on the blanket. She pawed at the blanket and walked around in a circle three or four times then finally laid down on her bed to take a nap.

When suppertime came, Half Pint put out a bowl of food for his new companion. The hungry pup ran toward the food.

Just as she put her head down to get her first bite, out ran two tiny alligators! They were headed for Nicky's food. Nicky jumped back.

Then Half Pint stepped in and fussed at the alligators for being rude to their new roommate.

"Don't be afraid, Nicky. These two little creatures won't hurt you – but they *will* eat your supper if you let them! They are baby alligators that got lost from their home. I'm sure you will become great friends," Half Pint said.

Then he turned to the little 'gators and said, "Hey, guys, let the new baby eat."

They moved away from the bowl, and Nicky gobbled down her supper.

After she had eaten, Half Pint took her outside to show her the swamp for the first time. It looked very different than anything she had ever seen on the farm. There were huge trees lining the banks of a large, dark body of water and big trees in the water reaching to the sky. The trees had long branches with grey moss hanging from them.

The sun was setting on the horizon, and the brilliant orange and purple sunset was being reflected in the water. Nicky could hear the sounds of birds and animals in the distance, singing, hooting and croaking.

They stayed outside admiring the beauty of the swamp until it got dark, then went back into the houseboat for the night.

Nicky went straight to her bed and fell fast asleep. She was awakened by the two baby alligators trying to get into her bed. She didn't seem to mind having company, so her first night in her new home was spent sleeping with alligators. 🐾

CHAPTER TWO

Learning About the Swamp

*T*he next morning the little dog woke to the quacking of ducks and the honking of geese. It sounded like morning on the farm. She jumped up and ran to the screen door. There was a family of ducks playing on one side of the houseboat and two big geese splashing around in the water on the other side.

"Well, Nicky, it's time for you to see the swamp for yourself. We'll go out in our boat, and I'll show you what I call 'the great outdoors.' Our other babies are going to stay home while you come with me."

Nicky followed Half Pint, staying close to his heels. She didn't want to lose him. They got into a small metal boat with two motors on the back.

As Half Pint turned on the motors, Nicky jumped on the seat next to him and snuggled up

Many ducks and geese can be found frolicking in the water and on the shore near Nicky's houseboat.

Nicky gets her first close-up look at the swamp as she stands on the bow of Half Pint's tour boat.

Half Pint's tour boat

An alligator suns itself on the bank of a bayou.

to his soft, wooly coat. The boat moved away from the dock then began to go faster and faster. Nicky's ears blew in the wind like two little black flags as the boat zipped along in the dark brown water. The boat made its way into a wide lake. Nicky could see several boats with people fishing near the shore of the lake. One of the boats was next to a big patch of bright green water lilies.

Half Pint's boat crossed the lake and turned in to a little bayou, then headed for a spot in the shade. He turned off the motors, and the boat glided quietly toward the bank.

Nicky was very alert, looking all around at trees and bushes such as she had never seen before.

"You see that big log right over there, Nicky?" Half Pint asked, as he pointed to an adult alligator sunning itself on the bank of the bayou.

Nicky looked in the direction of where Half Pint was pointing.

"That's no log. That's a grown-up alligator. It's got great big teeth and powerful jaws. It can eat a little dog like you in just one bite. So you must never, ever get close to one of those things. They can be very dangerous. Understand?"

Nicky looked at Half Pint as though she understood.

"Now, look over here," Half Pint said, pointing to what looked like a huge pile of sticks. "That's a beaver's den. That's where beavers live."

As Half Pint was talking, a large white bird, bigger than any Nicky had ever seen on the farm, glided right over the boat. Its wings were very long, and it flew so close to Nicky that she could almost feel its beautiful white feathers.

An egret searches for insects and small fish to eat. ➤

"That's an egret, Nicky. You'll see them everywhere you go in the swamp," Half Pint explained.

Nicky watched the great white bird as it landed in the shallow water near the beaver's den.

"Nicky, I want you to understand that my job is to take people around the swamp and show them all the animals and the beautiful scenery. I'm a swamp guide. And you will be my assistant swamp guide. It'll be your job to help entertain our guests."

The little assistant swamp guide didn't understand what Half Pint was trying to tell her. All she knew for sure was that she liked being with her new master in the great outdoors. And she seemed to be very interested in the egret that was now pecking in the bushes near the bank of the bayou, trying to find something to eat. 🐾

CHAPTER THREE

Nicky Goes to School

In addition to introducing Nicky to alligators, egrets and beavers, Half Pint taught her to do many things in the first year they were together – such as chasing away snakes and rescuing lost nutria. He even taught her how to play with baby alligators without hurting them.

Now, Nicky is a Rat Terrier, and her natural instinct is to track down rats and mice and kill them. But Half Pint has taught her not to hurt the animals she finds. He has taught her not to harm any creature smaller or weaker than her.

All Half Pint has to say is, "Good baby, good baby," and Nicky understands she is not to harm the little critter. Nutria, beaver and owls are "good babies." Snakes and rats are "bad babies," and they had better watch out for Nicky now that she is grown up and well trained!

When Half Pint is teaching Nicky to do some-

◄ *A stand of cypress trees in the Atchafalaya Basin serves as a haven for many kinds of feathered and furry forms of wildlife.*

thing he will show her how it is to be done. For example, he taught Nicky to check out the tour boat in the morning to make sure no snakes or rats had gotten in during the night. To do this, he would go into the boat, lift the gas tank and look around the boat for any "bad babies." While doing this, he would say, "Check it out. Check it out." If he saw a snake or rat he would shout, "Bad baby!" and poke at it with a stick and chase it out of the boat.

Nicky paid close attention to Half Pint as he demonstrated how to check out the boat. And she understood exactly what to do.

Today, when Half Pint says, "Check it out," Nicky jumps into the boat and looks all around. If she spots a "bad baby," she growls and barks and chases it out of the boat.

In a similar way, Half Pint taught Nicky to "check out" a beaver den to see if there were any beavers inside. He would jump off the tour boat and swim or wade to the den. Then he'd climb onto the den and look into the entranceway and ask, "Any-body home?"

Now, all he has to do is stop the boat and tell Nicky, "Go check it out." Nicky then jumps off the boat and swims to the den. When Half Pint asks, "Anybody home?" Nicky goes into the entranceway to see if there are any beavers inside. If they are there, they come running out as the adventurous little swamp dog barks and barges into their home. This gives the tourists on the tour boat a chance to see the beavers and to take pictures of them.

Half Pint has also taught Nicky never to get into a boat or car with a stranger unless he (Half Pint) gets in first. If someone besides Half Pint is carrying Nicky and begins walking toward a car or boat, Nicky will wiggle and scratch until she escapes.

Half Pint has taught Nicky these and many other lessons, because he loves this little dog who has become his constant companion. He thinks of Nicky as his best friend. 🐾

◄ *Nicky is a good pupil. She pays close attention when Half Pint is teaching her.*

Nicky checks out a beaver den to see if anyone is home.

Half Pint has taught Nicky not to harm any creatures smaller or weaker than her, including baby alligators. She plays with them without hurting them.

CHAPTER FOUR

Saving Miss Nicky

Nicky and Half Pint went out into the swamp early one morning just to scout around and to have some fun.

Half Pint spotted a group of baby alligators near the bank of a bayou and landed the boat nearby so Nicky could play with them. Nicky had been taught to be gentle with the little creatures. They were "good babies."

Nicky jumped off the boat into the water to play while Half Pint kept an eye on the mother alligator. She was on the other side of the bayou, on the opposite bank, watching her little ones closely. She was not happy to see the visitors.

Half Pint got out of the boat and began searching around the bank for alligator eggs. He wasn't looking at the mother alligator when she glided into the water without making a sound and

◄ *An egret keeps a lookout in alligator territory deep in the Atchafalaya swamp.*

began swimming rapidly toward Nicky.

Half Pint saw the mother alligator when she got close to Nicky. He came running along the bank, grabbed Nicky, and leaped into the boat in a flash! Just a few seconds later, the big, angry alligator jumped on the exact spot where Nicky had been playing. Mud and water splashed all over Nicky and Half Pint.

Half Pint put Nicky under his coat and hugged her. He knew the little dog could have been eaten by that huge alligator if he hadn't gotten to Nicky when he did.

Nicky learned a valuable lesson that day. Since then she has always been careful when she is around grown-up alligators, especially when their young are nearby. 🐾

Left: *Baby alligators swim near the bank of a bayou in the Atchafalaya Basin.*
Middle: *Nicky swims toward the little 'gators so she can play with them.*
Right: *Nicky searches for the 'gators, who seem to be playing hide-and-seek with her.*

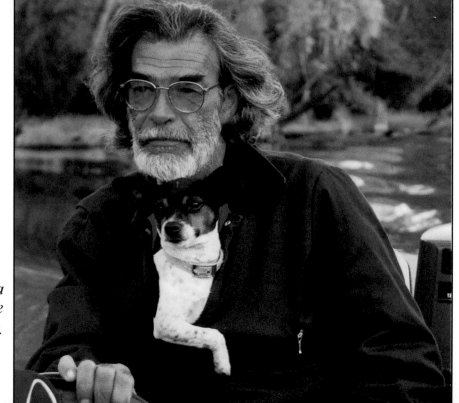

After nearly getting eaten by a big alligator, Nicky rides home under Half Pint's coat.

CHAPTER FIVE

Furry Friends

One summer afternoon when Half Pint and Nicky were riding around the swamp, Half Pint spotted a lost animal and pulled over to the bank.

"Stay here, Nicky," he said. "I have to pick up a little lost critter."

Nicky stood on the boat's seat and watched as Half Pint went to the edge of the woods then came walking back with something furry and brown wrapped in a blanket.

"It's a good baby, Nicky, *good baby*," he said. "Don't hurt it."

Nicky could smell a familiar odor coming from the bundle Half Pint was carrying as he set it down on the floor of the boat. She was very curious to see what her master had rescued this time.

"We're heading back to the houseboat, Nicky,"

◄ *Moss-draped cypress trees are among the most distinctive characteristics of the Atchafalaya swamp.*

A young beaver lost from her mother, such as this one, was rescued by Half Pint and later returned to her natural habitat.

Half Pint said as he cranked up the motors and backed away from the bank.

The wind blew Nicky's ears as she stared at the blanket with the little critter inside. When they got home, Half Pint picked up the bundle and took it into the houseboat. Nicky followed closely on his heels.

Then Half Pint unwrapped the blanket.

"This is a baby beaver that was lost from her mother," Half Pint said. "You have to take care of her just like I take care of you. She is a good baby, so you must be gentle with her. Okay?"

Nicky came over and licked Half Pint's hand, as if to say, "Okay. I understand."

In a few minutes Half Pint put the brown ball of fur on Nicky's bed. Nicky sniffed the damp little thing. It smelled like the swamp. She climbed onto her bed and snuggled up next to her new furry friend.

Nicky seemed to love the animal babies of the swamp – even the two little alligators that never stopped running all over the houseboat and jumping in and out of her water bowl.

The next morning Half Pint took Nicky and her furry friend all around the swamp, searching for the baby beaver's mother. They spent all day in the boat looking for a beaver den that seemed familiar to the little critter.

Finally, at sundown, they came across a big, fat mother beaver and three babies. The little brown baby got very excited and started to squeak, "Eee! Eee!" Half Pint washed it off in the swamp water and gently pushed it toward its mom. It made Half Pint feel good to help the little critter find its way home.

Just a few weeks later, it was Nicky's turn to be the hero. While on a swamp tour, she found an injured baby nutria that had been separated from his mother. Nicky brought the nutria back to the boat, gently carrying him in her teeth, as a mother dog would carry a young puppy. Half Pint praised Nicky for her good deed, then they took the baby home with them so they could nurse him back to good health.

Half Pint named the new baby Yaya. The little nutria slept with Nicky. When he wanted to swim he would get in Nicky's water bowl and splash around. This was a signal for Nicky to take him outside, so they would go outside and swim together in the water close to the houseboat.

It was plain to see that Nicky enjoyed swimming with Yaya. It was as though Yaya was her little brother, her favorite playmate.

Nicky plays with her friend, the beaver, on the dock near Half Pint's houseboat.

Nicky's friend, Yaya, is a young nutria that gets in Nicky's water bowl and just sits there. This is Yaya's way of telling Nicky that he wants to go outside for a swim.

Nicky seems a little frustrated when Yaya gets in her water bowl. She doesn't like to drink the water once Yaya bathes in it!

Nicky dries Yaya with her tongue once she is able to chase him out of her water bowl. Then they both get wet again just a few minutes later when they go outside to swim near the houseboat.

Yaya became a permanent resident of Half Pint's and Nicky's houseboat – though most of the animals they have taken in have been returned to the wilds. Nicky becomes attached to all her furry and feathered friends who come to live with her. If she had her way, none of the little critters would ever be returned home to live in the swamp. Then the houseboat would be like a zoo!

But Half Pint has to have some rules to maintain order in the houseboat. And the main rule is that once an animal from the wilds is grown up enough or well enough to survive on its own, he sets it free. He feels this is the natural thing to do. 🐾

CHAPTER SIX

Feathered Friends

One day a batch of ducklings was hatched near the houseboat, and Nicky decided to claim them as her own. She rounded up all ten of the yellow and black ducklings and began to lick them dry.

She wanted to bring them into the houseboat but it was already a little crowded with several other babies – two small alligators, a parrot and a pair of doves. Nicky led all the ducklings through her doggie door into the houseboat. She looked up at Half Pint as if to ask, "Please, can they come in and play?" Half Pint knew how much Nicky loved raising babies, so he let her keep them in a large tub inside. Each night Nicky curled up with the ducklings and slept with them.

In the mornings she would lead them out through her doggie door and take them for a swim. She would get in the water with the ducklings to

◄ *Roseate spoonbills survey the water for crawfish, minnows and the like.*

31

be sure they learned to swim. Then she would dry them off with her tongue.

While she was raising the ducklings, Nicky also had two doves, Cooie and Looie. They flew around the houseboat and often rode on Nicky's back. When Cooie and Looie would have babies they would build a nest inside their cage. Nicky would spend many hours with her head inside the cage waiting for the eggs to hatch. The minute they hatched Nicky would wash the new baby birds with her tongue. Cooie and Looie allowed Nicky to do this because they must have trusted her not to harm the new babies.

Another feathered friend that lived in the houseboat was an African Gray parrot named Benny Joe. Half Pint didn't find him in the swamp, but bought him at a pet shop. Benny Joe would sit on top of his cage chattering away and making noises that

sounded like a telephone ringing. Nicky and the parrot spent many hours playing on the floor of the houseboat after supper.

When Half Pint felt they'd had enough fun for one night, he would tell Nicky to send Benny Joe home. Nicky would obey: She'd growl at Benny Joe, bark at him and nudge him with her nose. The parrot would then go to his cage and wouldn't come out until morning. 🐾

Nicky checks on her adopted ducklings. At night she would curl up and sleep with them in the tub, as though she was their mother.

Cooie the dove lands on Nicky's back before getting a ride around the houseboat.

Nicky supervises as her adopted ducklings swim near the houseboat.

After playing with Benny Joe the parrot after supper, Nicky lets him know that the fun is over and it's time to go to his cage for the night. Nicky does this by barking at him and nudging him with her nose.

CHAPTER SEVEN

Show Time!

I n addition to helping Half Pint rescue lost or injured animals, Nicky's job is to help entertain the visitors who ride on the tour boat seeking an adventure in the swamp. She's the "assistant swamp guide."

Nicky's favorite game is finding a beaver's den. She knows when the motors of the boat stop running it's time to show off for the tourists. Quick as a wink, Nicky jumps off the boat and swims to the beaver house, hoping to find beavers to show the tourists.

She makes her way inside the beaver house to scout around. Then Half Pint says, "Anyone home, girl?" If there are beavers inside Nicky will bark, and they will run out of the house. When they do, everyone gets the chance to take pictures of the beavers.

◁ *An egret glides into the depths of the Atchafalaya swamp.*

Nicky spots a beaver's den ...

... she prepares to dive off the boat ...

... she splashes into the water ...

The visitors love to watch Nicky swimming with the beavers and baby alligators, especially when she brings a baby in her mouth over to the boat for people to see up close.

Nicky seems to enjoy having her picture taken and pleasing the visitors. She knows when they want to photograph her. She actually poses for the cameras!

This little swamp dog is really something to see, doing all her tricks, especially when she takes a flying leap off the moving boat and runs down the bank of the bayou trying to beat the boat to the beaver den.

Of all the tourists who come to visit Half Pint and Nicky, it is the children whom Nicky gets along with best. They play with her and rub her ears, and she makes them laugh by licking their faces.

Hundreds of children have visited Nicky in her home in the swamp. Many children get to visit the houseboat, too, and to meet several of Nicky's furry and feathered friends who live there. 🐾

... she swims toward the den ...　　　*... she barks when she gets close to the den...*　　　*... the adult beavers run out of their den.*

Nicky is held by Lindsey Breaux of Lafayette, La., one of many children who have enjoyed the company of the little swamp dog while touring the Atchafalaya Basin.

Half Pint and Nicky have helped all sorts of lost or injured swamp animals, including owls, raccoons, ducklings and even the rare osprey.

*H*aving been together for several years now, Half Pint and Nicky continue riding around in the Atchafalaya River swamp.

If you're in the area, you'll recognize them when you see a small, black and white and brown dog sitting next to a nice man with a silver beard. On cold days Nicky will be wearing a little red sweater, given to her by a lady from Lafayette who admires her a lot.

Half Pint and Nicky spend most days out in the swamp, saving lost critters and helping visitors to appreciate the beauty of the great outdoors. 🐾

Glossary

Basin: A tract of land drained by a river and its tributaries. (The Atchafalaya River Basin – which includes swamps, lakes, bayous and canals – runs from central Louisiana to the southern part of the state and empties into Atchafalaya Bay, which is a part of the Gulf of Mexico. The basin is 17 miles wide (on average) and about 75 miles long, running north-and-south.

Beaver: A furry rodent with a wide, flat tail that looks like a paddle. The beaver is known for its ability to cut down trees with its strong front teeth. It lives in rivers, streams and freshwater lakes, including those of the Atchafalaya Basin. It can hold its breath for 15 minutes and swim underwater for half a mile.

Egret: A tall, usually white bird with long legs, a long neck and long, thin bill that feeds on small fish, crawfish and insects. The egret is seen throughout the swamps and wetlands of Louisiana and in other parts of the U.S. as far north as the Great Lakes. Snowy Egrets and Great Egrets are the types most often seen in the Atchafalaya Basin. Adults range from 19 to 40 inches long and have a wingspread of up to 67 inches.

Great Egret

Snowy Egret

Houseboat: A small house that is attached to and sits on a barge. A houseboat floats on water and usually can be moved from one place to another. (Half Pint and Nicky live in a houseboat.)

Levee: A continuous dike or ridge of earth designed to confine water and thus prevent flooding. (The levees which run parallel to the Atchafalaya River were built to keep the river's floodwaters from reaching south Louisiana farms and towns.)

Nutria: A large aquatic rodent that resembles a beaver. It has brown fur, small ears, webbed hind feet and a long, rat-like tail. The nutria is an excellent swimmer; it eats mostly water plants and lives along the banks of lakes and streams, including those of the Atchafalaya Basin.

Swamp: Wet, spongy land saturated and sometimes covered with water. (The Atchafalaya swamp is filled with crawfish, alligators, ducks, and wildlife of every description, as well as moss-draped cypress trees, willows and a wide variety of other plant life.

Sources: The World Book Encyclopedia and Webster's New Collegiate Dictionary
Illustrations by Brion Angers, Lafayette, La.